WHAT IF
YOUR TEEN
ISN'T THE
PROBLEM

A GUIDE TO CONSCIOUS PARENTING

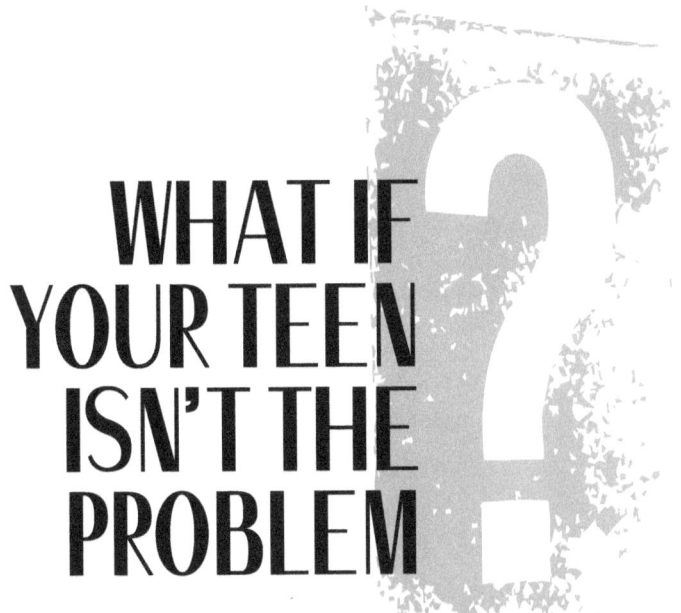

WHAT IF
YOUR TEEN
ISN'T THE
PROBLEM

A GUIDE TO CONSCIOUS PARENTING

BY DEBRA BECK

What If Your Teen Isn't The Problem?
A Guide To Conscious Parenting
By Debra Beck

© 2025 Debra Beck
EmpoweredTeensandParents.com
SedonaSoulRetrieval.com
Published in Sedona, AZ

Published by DJB Creations
in affiliation with Fearless Literary Services

ISBN: 979-8-218-66791-7

Library of Congress Control Number:
2025911956

Book and Cover Design: Jane Perini,
www.thundermountaindesign.com

Production and Management:
D. Patrick Miller Fearless Literary
www.fearlessbooks.com/Literary.html

ACKNOWLEDGMENTS

I am deeply grateful to all the teachers and mentors in my life who have guided me through my own healing journey. Their wisdom and support have helped me navigate childhood trauma, allowing me to do what I love with clarity and purpose—helping parents and teens.

Two of my greatest organic teachers are my daughters. Their presence continually reveals my blind spots and areas for growth, and I am endlessly thankful for the lessons they bring into my life.

A special thank you to Jane Perini for her creative vision in making this book visually appealing and to Karen Reider for her unwavering support from start to finish. Thanks to D. Patrick Miiler of Fearless Literary for help at the final stages of production and launch.

And finally, to all my clients—thank you for embracing this work, for showing up for your children, and for making a meaningful impact in the world. Your courage and commitment inspire me every day.

CONTENTS

FOREWORD · 8

INTRODUCTION · 11

CHAPTER ONE · 17
Do Your Wounds Get in the Way

CHAPTER TWO · 23
Getting to Know Your Old Beliefs from the
Lens of Your Inner Child

CHAPTER THREE · 31
Feeling Your Feelings and Doing Your Inner Work

CHAPTER FOUR · 35
Allow and Love Me for Being Me

CHAPTER FIVE · 43
Are You Being Authentic?

CHAPTER SIX · 49
Communication, Can You Hear Me?

CHAPTER SEVEN · 57
Boundaries — A Framework for Growth

CHAPTER EIGHT · 65
Respect: A Two-Way Street

CHAPTER NINE · 69
Honesty, Integrity, and the Power of Your Word

CHAPTER TEN · 75
Mistakes: Opportunities for Growth, Not Just Punishment

CHAPTER ELEVEN · 81
Security and Self-Confidence:
Building a Strong Foundation

CHAPTER TWELVE · 85
Positivity Versus Negativity

CHAPTER THIRTEEN · 89
Teen Sexuality

CHAPTER FOURTEEN · 95
The Digital World

CHAPTER FIFTEEN · 101
Rebuilding Trust

CHAPTER SIXTEEN · 107
Healing Yourself and Your Children — It's All about You

RESOURCES · 110
Resources from Debra for Continued Growth
and Other Helpful Resources

FOREWORD

Heal your relationship with your teenager by healing yourself. No, it's not as simple as it sounds, but it's not difficult either. I know, because I've succeeded at this by working with Debra Beck throughout my daughter's teen years. The process is challenging at times, but is also wonderful, magical work that will change your life for the better, not to mention the life of your blossoming young adult. In fact, I continue to work with Debra to keep my old, erroneous beliefs at bay.

In *What if Your Teen Isn't the Problem?* you'll learn the tools to look deeply inward before reacting outwardly. Debra illuminates some of the common wounds we adults have experienced as children and how to make peace with them, thereby being able to lead our children with our current wisdom, and not our muddied past. As Debra illustrates in one of her easy-to-understand, interactive chapters, I was able to identify being the product of one parent who pushed me to be a high achiever (which was where I saw my value) and the other who was working and unavailable much of the time. Debra uncovered that I hadn't experienced love for who I was, but what I did, which caused me to be a classic people pleaser.

My daughter, who is now almost 30, was the opposite; she was headstrong, self-assured, and not fueled by praise, which put us in a cycle of conflict. When Debra worked with us, a light was shone on my outdated beliefs, which allowed me to see my daughter in a new way—with understanding, admiration and awe as she forged her own path, not the shadow path of her mother or father.

What if Your Teen Isn't the Problem? clearly outlines all you'll need to know to untangle old emotions and beliefs. You'll learn the difference between reacting and responding, and tools for when you simply need to take a breather before engaging in a situation with your teenager, keeping it civil and not volatile. By dealing with the feelings that have been stuffed long ago, you can become a stable, loving, supportive parent to your child. Overcome the uncomfortable and make the changes suggested in Debra's book. You'll be proud you did this life-changing work!

Dina Ruiz Eastwood
Writer, News Anchor
Client since 2011

INTRODUCTION

Her childhood and teen years were riddled with anxiety and feelings of separation. She felt disconnected, unsafe, confused, and very lonely. Growing up was a frightening experience, leaving her with a constant sense that something was wrong—that she wasn't right. Because her parents were unable to deal with their own childhood traumas and were so disconnected from themselves, it was impossible for them to provide a safe home environment. Her teenage years and adulthood were full of trauma and misunderstanding, making success an uphill battle. That was me.

Life is difficult for teens, and without parental support, it can be excruciating. It is critical for teens to feel safe and connected to their parents in order to navigate the challenges of today's world. Ninety percent of the teens I have spoken to say they don't feel connected to their parents and wish they had a closer relationship with them.

What If Your Teen Isn't the Problem? shows parents how important it is to work through their own childhood wounds before they can create a healthy environment where their children can blossom into self-assured, independent young adults who are able to follow their own passions and dreams. Parents who commit to working through their inner-child wounds will start responding to their teens instead of reacting out of fear.

Parents want to be connected with their teens so they can be the ones influencing and guiding them. The biggest concern for parents is that their teens are not talking to them. Instead, they seek guidance from their friends. This terrifies parents, as it should.

What If Your Teen Isn't the Problem? provides clear, concise examples through real-life experiences and scenarios of how reacting versus responding plays out in different parent-teen interactions.

In my 30 years of mentoring teens, I have realized that a teen's behavior will shift only when parents acknowledge how their own unresolved fears and wounds shape their reactions to their children. If parents have not addressed their own childhood issues, they will unknowingly project their fears onto their teens, leading to disconnection and shutdown.

When you were a child, how did you feel? Did you feel supported by your parents? Did you feel they truly saw you for who you were? Did they listen to you? Encourage you? Or were you ignored? Some of you may have been controlled so tightly that you couldn't breathe, while others had to raise themselves. Perhaps you were one of the lucky few whose parents truly showed up for them.

In my childhood I felt disconnected, separate, and deeply lonely. The anxiety that followed me through my adolescence was almost unbearable. Because my parents were so disconnected from themselves, I never felt safe or truly connected at home. Everyone pretended that everything was okay. But I knew it wasn't.

My mother was very reclusive, just getting by in life—a shell of a person. As a child, I would look into her eyes and see the pain she carried. I saw the darkest parts of her soul, desperate for any sense of normalcy. She lost her mother at a young age and was raised by her father and a stepmother who treated her poorly.

My father was a tough man, hiding behind the pain of losing his own mother, who took her life when he was only two years old. His father, unable to cope, gave him up to foster care at four. As an adult, my sister once asked him to answer some genealogy questions, one of which was, "What was your biggest regret in life?" His answer: "Not having any love in my life as a child." Reading that made my heart ache and gave me deep compassion for him.

I felt invisible to my parents, lost in their unresolved pain. I don't blame them—I know they did the best they could. But because they had not done their own inner work, they could not be present for me.

I do know that my life would have been much easier and more nurturing if my parents had been able to show up for me. Instead, I faced the world feeling scared and unsure of myself. Making decisions was excruciating, and even now, remnants of those insecurities linger in certain situations.

I share my childhood story because it is a perfect example of how unhealed parental wounds affect children long into adulthood. Some parents may never do the inner work necessary to heal, simply because they lack awareness. My parents never had the consciousness to even recognize their emotional wounds. But these were my lessons to learn, so I could show up differently in the world.

If you yearn for a deeper, more connected relationship with your teen, this is a powerful path to get there. I have seen parent-child relationships shift in miraculous ways—including in my own life with my daughters.

When I became a parent, I knew that to show up for my girls the way they needed me to, I had to first understand myself. My journey of self-discovery was the key to connecting with my daughters in a profound way.

So began my journey through the depths of the pain and darkness I had carried for years—pain that had prevented me from showing up fully for myself, my children, and the world. There was no other path but through the pain of past wounds in order to reach a place of love within myself.

My daughters are now in their late forties, each walking their own paths and learning their own lessons. Everything unfolded exactly as it was meant to traveling this journey together.

This is your opportunity to reflect on your own childhood, to see how your experiences have shaped you, and to recognize your role in your relationship with your teen. By healing what you can within yourself, you can create a more connected, fulfilling relationship with your teen—and with everyone in your life.

I wasn't a perfect parent, but through my years of self-discovery, I have developed a deep connection with my daughters, and I know that without doing my own inner work, I wouldn't be able to experience this closeness with them.

When I first started mentoring teens, I knew that real progress could only happen when their parents were willing to do their own emotional work. If parents react to their teens from a place of unhealed pain, there is no room for true connection and understanding.

Have you ever found yourself in an argument with your teen where nothing seems to get resolved? You just keep coming back to the same frustration. I call this the "spin class" of parenting—you're pedaling fast but going nowhere. It's great for endless quarreling but terrible for building connection.

Here's what's actually happening: Your teen does something they're not supposed to. You get triggered, take it personally, and react. You believe they've let you down, and your disappointment is projected onto them. You think they are the cause of your disappointment. When you blame them for how you feel, you then feel the need to control their behavior to make yourself feel better. Instead of realizing that they are triggering an old wound from your own childhood, you react, and the cycle continues. The result? A shut-down teenager who feels unheard and misunderstood.

But when you recognize your trigger as *your own* and stop projecting it onto your teen, you free up the energy of blame. You can then show up differently in that moment, creating space for understanding and connection.

If you're looking for a more conscious, loving, and authentic way to connect with your teen, I assure you that turning inward is the place to start. If you are ready to make this shift, know that your commitment to your own healing will benefit everyone in your life.

I commend you for being here. This journey is happening for you at the perfect time.

Many of the struggles between parents and teens stem from unexamined emotional triggers, past wounds, fears, or learned behaviors.

> *"Until you make the unconscious conscious,*
> *it will direct your life and you will call it fate."*
>
> — CARL JUNG

CHAPTER ONE

Do Your Wounds Get in the Way?

W hat does parenting look like? What does it mean to be a parent? We bring these amazing little people into the world, and I'm not sure we fully realize the magnitude of our responsibility to them.

Everyone has different ideas about what makes a good parent, but many of the core objectives are universal. We want our children to grow up to be confident, happy adults with a strong sense of self, making good decisions for themselves. That is our goal in a nutshell, right? The question is: as parents, what can we do to help them get there?

Looking back on my childhood, one of the biggest obstacles I faced was my parents' inability to do what was necessary to help me become a confident, happy person with healthy self-esteem. They hadn't worked through their own childhood wounds, which made it impossible for them to be emotionally available to me. They were completely shut down, trapped behind the doors of their own childhood pain. If we are shut down in any area of our lives, parenting becomes really tough. Why? If we haven't worked through our own childhood wounds or at least gained awareness of them, we tend to react out of fear instead of responding with a compassionate heart.

In every chapter, I will discuss the key differences between reacting and responding. When we react, it's because we are triggered by something that taps into an old wound. Someone does or says something that makes us angry, sad, hurt, or afraid, and we slip into our wounded child. Once we are in that wounded state, all we can do is react. If you look at your behavior when you've been triggered, you'll notice that you often act just like a child, perhaps yelling, crying, or feeling overwhelmed with anxiety. You might even storm out of the room—a clear indication that your wounded child is activated.

If you can become keenly aware of your triggers when they happen and take a step back, you have a better chance of responding instead of reacting.

The next time someone upsets you, pay close attention to how you act. Try stepping outside of the situation, either physically or emotionally. Usually, we are so deep inside our wounds that we don't even realize we are overreacting and blaming the other person for how we feel. Our goal is to recognize our triggers before they hijack us. You can stop a knee-jerk reaction by first becoming aware of it, pausing, and then shifting your focus to your emotions. The more awareness you develop around your childhood wounds, the better you'll be at recognizing them when they're activated.

With conscious parenting comes the responsibility to do your own inner work. When you work through your wounds, you can stay open, remain in your heart, and be emotionally available for your teen in a whole new way. This journey is about knowing yourself so you can be present for your children and others in a more loving, compassionate way.

We want to respond to our teens in a loving, caring way. When we react instead, our children often feel misunderstood or unheard. When we are reacting from a wounded place, we aren't truly present for their needs or emotions. In a triggered state, our wounded inner child is focused only on its own pain, making it impossible to show up for anyone else.

The truth is your kids are one of the greatest indicators of your emotional growth. They serve as a barometer, reflecting where you still have work to do. Throughout this book, we will explore your childhood wounds so you can better understand yourself, and in turn, be more emotionally available for both yourself and your children.

As I continued my own personal growth, I noticed a shift. I wasn't reacting as much, not just with my kids but also with the people around me. The more I processed my childhood wounding, the better I felt in the world, and the more I was able to show up for myself and others—especially my children.

When we contract from being triggered, it doesn't matter who or where the trigger comes from—our teens, other family members, friends, co-workers, or even our own thoughts—the reaction is always rooted in unhealed wounds that need to be examined. If you pay attention, you'll notice that every emotional contraction can be traced back to a childhood wound.

The process outlined in this book will help you stop taking things so personally, identify where your triggers come from, and develop the tools to pause, breathe, and respond from a loving place.

The more you understand and heal your childhood wounds, the more emotionally available you will become for your children.

This book is designed to help you develop the tools you need to support your kids by showing up for yourself in a whole new way.

One of the most important tools to develop is learning how to observe your reactions from an outside perspective. Without training, when we are caught in the wounds of our childhood, we are completely consumed by our emotions, making it difficult to step back and gain clarity. Most of the time, when we get triggered, we automatically slip into childhood wounding. If we can't recognize what's happening, we end up reacting from our wounded inner child instead of responding from our adult self.

Hopefully, you are up for the task. It's not an easy journey, but it is deeply fulfilling. Doing this work leads to a stronger, more connected relationship with yourself and your teen while also helping them develop a deeper connection to themselves.

When I reflect on my relationship with my daughters today, compared to where I was before I did my inner work, I recognize a significant difference. The feeling of being disconnected from your teen is overwhelming—the pain can feel like your heart is breaking. I remember the guilt I felt, the constant thought that I should be able to do better, but at the time, I simply didn't know how.

It wasn't until I turned inward, examined my reactions, and worked through my wounds that I was able to approach parenting from a place of compassion—for myself, my children, and others.

The best part of this healing journey is that it allows you to put an end to your regrets and guilt. You can finally know, deep in your heart, that you are doing everything in your power to be a better parent and person. And in doing so, your healing will help your teen heal as well.

If you are willing to embark on this journey of self-discovery, and if you can acknowledge that you play a significant role in the disharmony between you and your teen, then there is a real opportunity to heal and cultivate a deeper, more authentic relationship with your teen.

I talk to so many parents who are focused on getting their kids to change but don't recognize their own profound role in the dynamic. Parenting doesn't work that way. It's not just your child who needs to shift—you have work to do as well.

This journey requires deep self-reflection, and it is a lifelong process. I have been doing self-discovery work for 30 years, using many different approaches, and I still slip into reaction mode sometimes. The difference now is that I can catch myself quickly and change direction.

If you, as a parent, don't change your reactive behavior, you will struggle to help your teen develop the tools they need. Only through your own commitment to self-awareness and healing can you truly transform your relationship with your teen. This will allow you to be emotionally available to them in a whole new way—helping them grow into strong, self-assured adults. The choice is yours. What direction will you take?

> *"Knowing yourself is the beginning*
> *of all wisdom."*
>
> —ARISTOTLE

Helping your teen understand themselves fosters wisdom, confidence, and the ability to navigate life with clarity.

Take a few moments and reflect on these questions:

- ◆ *What does your teen do that triggers you?*
- ◆ *How do you react?*
- ◆ *Does your reaction seem childish?*
- ◆ *Do you feel like you are right and they are wrong?*
- ◆ *What do you feel when this happens?*

CHAPTER TWO

Getting to Know Your Old Beliefs from the Lens of Your Inner Child

First and foremost, we need to figure out what beliefs you formed when you were a child. If you know what those are, you will know why your teen or others trigger you and can then examine how you might be acting out. When someone triggers you, it is because you're buying into a belief system that developed in your childhood. If you don't know what your belief systems are, then fear will come up and you will project it—blaming the person for how you feel, instead of recognizing that they are beliefs from an old story and turning inward.

When you were a child, things happened that were disturbing, and you created a story and belief around them. For example, my father was a binging alcoholic and my mother was fairly depressed. The lens my little girl saw things through, wasn't that something was wrong with them, but instead believed that something was wrong with her. The beliefs she created were: I'm not a priority, I'm not good enough, I'm not safe in the world, I can't trust people, I'm not considered, I'm always doing something wrong, and I'm unlovable. This perception came from the distorted lens of a very young child. Are these beliefs true? Or is the truth simply that my father was a binging alcoholic and my mother was fairly depressed due to their own wounding?

If I live my life through these beliefs—not being a priority, not being good enough, not being safe in the world, unable to trust people, not being considered and unlovable—then this is how the world will show up for me, especially with my family members. By buying into this belief system, and carrying it into adulthood, I fall into thinking that others make me feel like I'm not a priority, not good enough, and so on. This is where projection begins. If I believe you are the cause of my discomfort instead of recognizing it as my own wound, I will blame you, instead of realizing this belief originated in childhood. Instead, I must turn inward to heal it, feel what I need to feel, and not project it onto somebody else.

Before moving on, I would like you to create a list of emotional wounds from your childhood, and then, next to each wound, see if you can uncover what beliefs you may have created around those wounds as a child.

Here are a few examples of how painful childhood experiences can lead to limiting beliefs:

- **Parent was unpredictable due to drinking, temper, sickness, or mental illness – Possible beliefs:** I'm not safe in the world, I can't trust people, I'm not a priority, I'm not important, life is scary, I need to be a good girl/boy, I must not rock the boat, I have to walk on eggshells, grin and bear it, I'm always doing something wrong, I need to please, I don't matter, the unknown is scary, I'm not protected, I can't have boundaries, I'm not in control of my life, I need to fix things, life is confusing, I feel disconnected.

- **Parent worked a lot or was emotionally unavailable – Possible beliefs:** I'm not supported, I'm all alone in the world, I'm not safe, I'm not a priority, I'm not important, people are unavailable, I'm not seen, I don't deserve love, love is hard to get, I'm responsible for everything, I'm rejected, I feel disconnected, I am alone, I need to find happiness elsewhere.

- **Parent was really strict or pushed you to be a high achiever – Possible beliefs:** I'm not good enough, it's never enough, I'm not loved for who I am but only for what I do, there's something wrong with me, I'm always doing something wrong, I'm misunderstood, I'm not smart enough.

- **Parent favored or needed to attend to another sibling due to illness – Possible beliefs:** I'm not good enough, there's something wrong with me, my needs aren't as important as others', I'm not lovable, I'm not considered, I'm not heard or seen.

- **Parent was intrusive or too close – Possible beliefs:** I can't have boundaries, I'm not respected, I have no rights, other people's needs are more important than mine, I can't trust people, I'm trapped, I have no choice, I need to escape.

- **Parents arguing consistently – Possible beliefs:** The unknown is scary, I can't trust people, life is exhausting, life is confusing, life is scary, I'm always doing something wrong, I'm responsible for others' emotions, I need to fix things, grin and bear it, I must be a good girl/boy, I feel disconnected.

- **Infidelity – Possible beliefs:** I can't trust people, love is hard to get, life is confusing, I'm not safe in the world, I'm not in control of my life, I'm not a priority, I need to please.

- **Money struggles – Possible beliefs:** I'm not in control of my life, I need to fix things, money is hard to get, I have to work hard for money, I have to do something I don't love for money, I'm not worthy, life is scary, the unknown is scary, I'm inadequate, I don't deserve happiness or abundance, I'm not protected, life isn't fair.

When we understand how childhood wounds shaped our belief system, we can start noticing what triggers us today, especially with our teens. For instance, in my family, there was a lot of chaos, my mother definitely favored my sister, and no one ever talked about my father's drinking. My beliefs are that others are more important than me, I'm not considered, I'm always doing something wrong, and I'm unlovable. So, when something similar shows up in my adult life, for example, a friend excludes me, I feel a disturbance in my stomach because my little girl inside is reliving that old feeling of being unimportant, unlovable, doing something wrong and being overlooked. Because I know this about myself, I don't lash out at my friends and project my feelings onto them. I turn inward, and sit with my feelings, knowing they stem from childhood, and this situation is simply a mirror for my healing.

This understanding is crucial when your teen triggers you. Your triggers are not about them; they are echoes of your childhood wounds. Trying to get your teen to behave in a certain way so that you feel better only leads to resistance and emotional distance. If they shut down, they will not come to you when they're in need. Instead, they will seek guidance elsewhere—something no parent wants.

When you feel triggered, you want to respond with love, not react from fear. If you act out of your own wounds and old beliefs, you will react from a fearful state. But if you pause, breathe, and turn inward, recognizing where this discomfort comes from, you can approach them with love. Your child will feel the difference.

> *"Your own self-realization is the greatest service you can render the world."*
>
> — RAMANA MAHARSHI

When parents and teens embrace self-awareness, they build stronger relationships and set a positive example for the world around them.

Here's a real-life example from a client of mine, a mother. Her daughter came to her, concerned about a friend who had started vaping. Instantly, the mother became triggered, fearing that her daughter might start vaping, too. Instead of stepping into her daughter's reality, she projected her fears and reacted by saying,

"You're not vaping, are you? That's terrible for you!" Then she listed all the reasons vaping is bad. Most mothers would feel justified in their reaction, but all it did was shut her daughter down and disrupt any chance for meaningful communication.

If we look at the mother's beliefs, she may have been unconsciously reacting from: I need to fix everything, I'm not in control of my life, I'm responsible for everyone and everything, or the unknown is scary.

Had she recognized her trigger and taken ownership of her fear, her response might have been different. Imagine if, instead, she paused, grounded herself, and responded with curiosity: "I can see why this concerns you. How does it feel having a good friend do something that isn't good for her? Is there anything I can do to support you?"

One thing I know for sure: When you are triggered, you cannot think clearly. The calmer and more self-aware you are with your daughter, the more you empower her to make better decisions while strengthening your bond.

Take some time to reflect. Create a list of childhood hurts and the beliefs they may have formed. Then, notice what triggers you with your teen and connect the dots to your past. This awareness is where healing begins.

Take a few moments and reflect on these questions:

- *What old beliefs did you discover you have from the chapter?*
- *How do they show up with your teen?*
- *How do you behave when you are triggered?*

RESPOND OR REACT

◆ SITUATION ◆

Your teen doesn't follow through on taking the trash out.

◆ REACTION ◆

Nagging, yelling, or threatening consequences
out of frustration.

◆ POSSIBLE OLD BELIEFS ◆

I'm responsible for everything. I'm not appreciated. I'm
not respected. No one has regard for me. I don't matter.

◆ RESPONSE ◆

Instead of reacting emotionally, take a step back
and approach the situation calmly. Sit down with your
teen and explain the importance of being a team player.
Ask open-ended questions, like, "What's been making
this hard for you?" or "Is there something I can do to
support you in following through?" Acknowledge their
perspective, then ask what they think a fair consequence
should be if they don't follow through. Once an agreement is made, be consistent with the expectations
and follow-through.

CHAPTER THREE

Feeling Your Feelings and Doing Your Inner Work

I n the last chapter, you learned about the hurts from your childhood, the old beliefs attached to them, and the triggers that activate those old beliefs. It's crucial to identify these beliefs so you can catch yourself when your teen activates one or more of them. If you are unaware of these patterns, you will likely get hijacked by your emotions, react and project your feelings and fears onto them.

Once you have a clear understanding of your wounds and old beliefs, the next step is to identify what triggers them. A valuable exercise before moving forward is to list on a sheet of paper each old belief and, beneath it, write down what triggers it and how you typically react when it gets activated.

- ◆ Old belief:
- ◆ What triggers it, and how do you act out?

Do this exercise for each of your old beliefs from childhood. Once you have a clear list of your beliefs and their triggers, the next step is to focus on what you can do when those beliefs get activated.

The first thing you need to do is pause and slow down your mind and body. Take two deep breaths—one to relax your body and the other to open your heart space. Then, internally or aloud, acknowledge: "I am triggered." If your teen is aware that you are working on this, saying it aloud can be beneficial. The moment you recognize you're triggered, you activate a higher, more conscious part of yourself—the observer—rather than allowing your wounded inner child to take over. Mastering this one step alone can completely change the dynamic between you and your teen.

If you find that you cannot maintain a sense of calm in the moment, the best thing to do is remove yourself from the situation after first letting your teen (or whoever triggered you) know that you need to take a moment to breathe and regain composure. You can do this in a loving way by explaining, "I've been triggered, and I don't want to say or do anything that might harm our relationship. I need to step away and process this, and we will come back to it later."

A Format for Doing Your Inner Work

Once you are in a quiet space, breathe and regulate your body. Observe the story your mind is creating and how it aligns with your old beliefs. Either say aloud or write down which beliefs are being triggered. I highly recommend writing them at first until this process becomes second nature.

First state the trigger:

◆ My teen has attitude, my teen is on his devise all the

time, my teen lied to me, my teen consistently misses curfew, etc.

Then identify the old belief the trigger activated:

◆ I'm not respected, I'm not heard, I'm not considered, I can't have boundaries, list the ones you uncovered from list of old beliefs.

Then gently shift your focus to what you are feeling. It's essential to move slowly through this part and truly sit with your emotions. Common feelings that arise from triggers include:

◆ Frustration, anger, disappointment, sadness, shame, hopelessness, vulnerability, exhaustion, helplessness, worry, overwhelm, nervousness, anxiety, alarm, agitation, impatience, uneasiness, distress, confusion, upset, or resentfulness.

Once you identify what you are feeling, allow yourself to feel it fully. This is the most important part of healing childhood wounds. Many people avoid emotions at all costs. Just look at how often people turn to distractions—shopping, watching TV, scrolling social media, eating, venting to a friend—instead of facing their feelings. But real healing happens when you allow yourself to feel, even if it's uncomfortable.

Now, track how the sensation manifests in your body:

◆ Tightness in your chest? A sick feeling in your stomach? Tension in your neck? A headache? Simply observe where the emotion is stored in your body.

Then, notice what action you are being pulled toward:

- Do you feel the urge to yell at your teen? Explain repeatedly why they were wrong? Ground them without discussion? Walk away and give them the silent treatment?

To recap, the format for doing your inner work:

- The trigger is:
- The old beliefs are:
- The feelings are:
- The sensation in my body is:
- The action I want to take is:

By consistently using this format to track your triggers, beliefs, feelings, sensations in your body, and reactions, healing begins within yourself and with your teen.

When we project our feelings onto our teens, we do so to avoid feeling them ourselves. But projection leads to no healing, no growth, and no learning. Instead, it reinforces our old beliefs and shuts our teen out.

Use this framework throughout the week to track your triggers and begin shifting your behavior. Observe what shifts in your relationship when you make these changes.

"The wound is not my fault.
But the healing is my responsibility."

— MARIANNE WILLIAMSON

CHAPTER FOUR

Allow and Love Me for Being Me

Do we own our children? Are they ours? Yes, our children are born through us, but I do not believe that they are something we own. Khalil Gibran said, "You may give them your love, but not your thoughts, for they have their own thoughts. You may house their bodies, but not their souls, for their souls dwell in the house of tomorrow, which you cannot visit, not even in your dreams." This quote emphasizes that they are not our possessions but rather individuals with their own thoughts and destiny. They have their own spirit, and they are on their own journey. Our job is to love them unconditionally, let them be who they are, and help them become who they are meant to be so they can fulfill their purpose in life.

When we impose our opinions and judgments on them and try to control them, it is only because we have not dealt with our own fears stemming from our childhood wounds. This behavior only drives them further away from their true selves and, ultimately, from us. We need to get out of their way so they can blossom into the human beings they want to be, not who we need them to be.

Guidance is best given without having to take control of the situation. It means allowing your teen to safely explore who they are and who they want to be, while giving them the options they need to figure things out on their own. Encourage them in everything they do, even if it's not something you would do or believe in. It's not your job to tell them who to be.

When we impose our opinions and beliefs on our children, they start to resent us and shut us out. Once they shut down to us, we are no longer available to help them, to guide them, or to offer any assistance at all. They stop listening to us.

Have you ever met someone who lived the life their parents wanted them to live and ended up being miserable? I mentored a woman who told me that she was a doctor not because she wanted to be, not because she was passionate about it, and not because she wanted to help people. She became a doctor because her father wanted her to be one and because her father was one. When she looked at her life as a successful doctor, she was quite unhappy.

Now at 54 years old, she is changing her career because she no longer wants to live under her father's expectations. What a terrible injustice her father did to her. But before we start blaming her father, we must realize that he was acting out of his fears and his own childhood wounds. Obviously, she could have decided to change her path much earlier if she had done her inner work sooner. We do the inner work when we are ready, or in her father's case, not at all. We can take responsibility for our own lives at any point in adulthood. Although most of the time, we aren't connected enough to ourselves to even know how miserable we really are or how to take control of our own lives.

What we want to do is allow our children the freedom to explore the life they would choose to live, without letting our fears get in the way. Let them figure out their life's passions by supporting them, not telling them what to do, what to become, and how to become it.

"Be yourself; everyone else is already taken."

— OSCAR WILDE

As a parent, encourage your teen to embrace their individuality rather than comparing themselves to others. By modeling self-acceptance, you create a safe space for them to confidently express who they truly are. Let them know that their uniqueness is their greatest strength.

When we give our children the freedom to explore their lives at their own pace and avoid pushing them in any direction, we give them a priceless gift: the opportunity to find their place in life, their true passion, and their purpose. If we keep dragging them over to our dreams, which may be rooted in our fears, we take them off their true path.

Imagine your child happily walking barefoot down a beautiful, lush green path. They're smiling, skipping, and leaping in total bliss, when all of a sudden, they are snatched up harshly and thrown onto another path. This path doesn't feel the same; it has rocks and stickers that hurt them. They feel lost and disconnected on this path, but you keep telling them that it's a better path. They think, *How can it be better? It feels so wrong.* Can you see how this might teach your kids not to trust their own instincts? They know it feels crummy, and yet you're telling them it's better. Not only does this erode their confidence, but it also postpones their happiness.

So later in life, when your daughter is in a relationship with someone, she feels isn't right for her, but he keeps insisting, "No, no, we can make it work, we are perfect for each other," she will struggle to know what is right for her. She won't trust her own instincts. Do you want her to go through life ignoring her inner voice? It's hard to create the life you want when you are feeling off and disconnected. That's how we feel when we are not walking in our own truth. When we are truly doing what we are passionate about, we thrive.

As parents, we believe we know what is best for our kids, but how could we? We are not them, and it is not our path—it is theirs. So, as parents, can we allow our teens to be on their own path and just be there for them? Can we resist the urge to sway them in the direction we feel they need to go? Can we stop discouraging them with our judgments about the path they have chosen? Our judgments alone are enough to make them want to change paths. We are very influential—our words hold a lot of weight.

Think about a child going to their parent and saying, "Mom, I want to become an artist when I grow up," their face glowing with excitement. And the mother responds, "Lillie, that's foolish. Being an artist is a hobby, and they don't make any money. Besides, you're not that creative." OUCH! What would that do to that child's spirit? Crush it! What if that child had the potential to become the next Picasso, or to create art that healed people all over the world? But they never stepped into their dreams because their mother said it was foolish. Now imagine if, instead the mother said, "What a great idea! What type of artist do you want to become?" And then supported her child's exploration. Can you see how differently that might make a child feel? One way is completely disempowering, and the other is uplifting. One way disconnects the parent from the child; the other creates a stronger bond.

Everything we say to our kids from birth onward affects them—either negatively or positively. When they come to us with an idea, we can choose to say, "Wow, that's a great idea! You should explore it!" Then, they may discover it's not for them—or they may realize it's exactly what they want. This is part of figuring out who we are: exploring different aspects of life and seeing what resonates.

These two components are critical to practice when learning to connect with your children in a new way. First, get to know your own childhood wounds, so you can stop reacting through your own fears and instead start responding in a more compassionate, loving way. Second, realize that your children are individuals on their own path, here to experience their own lives and find their passion and purpose. Your job is to gently guide them on their path—not yank them off and force them onto yours.

You want to encourage them to be themselves. If they cannot be themselves around you, how will they ever know who they really are? They may always feel that something is wrong with them. After all, even their own parents don't accept them.

Our job is to help our children blossom into confident, self-assured individuals. If we accept our kids, love them exactly as they are, and support them on their journey, they will grow up learning to truly love themselves. Life is hard enough—even with the safety and support of your parents. Showing up for our teens in a healthy way is only possible if we are working through our own childhood wounds and doing our own healing.

Take a few moments and reflect on these questions:

- *In what ways do you push your teen instead of guide?*
- *In what way are you rooted in your fears?*
- *What can you do to start guiding your teen in a more conscious way?*
- *In what ways do you help your teen develop their passions?*

RESPOND OR REACT

◆ SITUATION ◆
Your teen is telling you she wants to be an influencer instead of going to college.

◆ REACTION ◆
Judgement through verbal criticism, saying it's not a real, sustainable career, shaming, and acting disgusted.

◆ POSSIBLE OLD BELIEFS ◆
People aren't realistic. I need to fix things. I need to protect. The unknown is scary. The worst will aways happen. I'm not heard.

◆ RESPONSE ◆
Always start with your inner work. Take a deep breath and realize that the more you push up against her, the more she will defend a bad position. Sit down with your teen and ask open-ended questions about what this looks like. Then possibly suggest she look at starting this now with your support and still go to college. The more you respond without fear and remain calm, the better chance you have of being heard.

CHAPTER FIVE

Are You Being Authentic?

When we are young, we have a keen sense of when people are being real or fake. We just feel it. Our intuition is still sharp and intact. However, when we live in a household where no one is being real and the family is pretending that everything is okay, it confuses our intuition—"okay" and "not okay" become entangled, making it hard to tell the difference.

When I was growing up, my father would go on drinking binges and come home screaming and throwing things. It was horrible and very scary for me as a child. My sister would pick me up and take me to the bathroom and say that everything was okay. I remember just staring at her in disbelief. *This is not okay!* would run through my head. I felt the wrongness in every part of my body. My whole being, especially my stomach, was saying that something was definitely wrong. To this day, I still feel situations that are off in my stomach, particularly while experiencing stress. Coincidence? I don't think so.

As I was growing up and becoming an adult, I never trusted my gut because throughout my childhood it was telling me something was wrong, while I was being told everything was fine by my entire family. My intuition was right on, but unfortunately discounted. By not discussing the issues at hand, they were implying that nothing was wrong. This created a total disconnect from my fundamental reality as a child.

If my parents had explained the situation to me, such as, "Your father is an alcoholic, and I'm struggling with depression, but we are getting help and doing the best we can," then at least my instincts would have been validated.

Obviously, that didn't happen because my parents didn't have the awareness to deal with their issues, much less bring them up with us. So, their issues remained unspoken, yet ever-present in our home. When these types of situations continue throughout our childhood, confusion with our feelings gets cemented. The more confused we get, the harder it becomes to connect with our true selves and trust our instincts as we grow older. That's why it's so important to be as authentic as possible with our children and to practice honesty, no matter how difficult the circumstances.

It's tough to be real with our feelings and let our children know when we're struggling. But if we want them to be honest about their problems, we must set the example. You don't have to go into detail and burden them, but don't pretend issues don't exist either. We must do our best to keep their intuition intact. The more honesty there is in the home, the better chance children will have at being in touch with their intuition—and this directly impacts their ability to develop a strong sense of self.

"Honesty and transparency make you vulnerable. Be honest and transparent anyway."

— MOTHER TERESA

As a parent, demonstrating honesty and transparency with your teen fosters trust and deepens your connection. Even when it feels uncomfortable or risky, being open shows them that vulnerability is a strength, not a weakness. Encouraging them to be honest without fear of judgment helps build a foundation of mutual respect and understanding.

One common and often unintentional display of dishonesty that parents may not be aware of starts when children are very young, saying, "Nothing is wrong." When a child sees their mother crying and asks, "What's wrong, Mommy?" and she replies, "Nothing," the child knows something is wrong. Validate their inner knowing—don't discount it. If you're crying and tell your child nothing is wrong, you're sending a mixed message that teaches them to doubt their intuition.

In my mentoring practice, I hear from parents who don't understand why their daughter is dating a jerk. "Why can't she tell the difference between a good guy and a bad guy?" Well, if a child's inner knowing is repeatedly dismissed throughout their childhood, they enter adolescence with weakened intuition, making it harder to discern good from bad, right from wrong.

When teens start dating and their boyfriend does something wrong, even if it feels off, they might not trust their instincts. Instead, they rationalize his behavior: "It's not that big of a deal. He treats me okay most of the time." Do you see the connection? If they are taught not to trust their inner feelings, this confusion will seep into all aspects of their lives.

This confusion can affect even the simplest or toughest decision—choosing a career, recognizing a healthy body image, or selecting friends and partners who treat them well. Feelings of doubt can lead to deep anxiety and insecurity.

For people to feel safe in the world, they need to trust themselves. To trust themselves, they must be connected to their intuition and believe in it.

We all have intuition, but do we listen to it? If our intuition isn't validated growing up, we struggle to connect with it as teens and adults. This is one of the biggest issues I see in adult women who have difficulty making healthy decisions. They agonize over the smallest choices, giving away their power to others, thinking others know better than they do.

One woman I mentored was married to a man who verbally abused her. When they argued, he would tell her he hated her and wanted a divorce. At first, she didn't even recognize this as inappropriate behavior or realize she didn't have to tolerate it. Her gut would sense something was off, but then she would justify his actions. So first, I had to help her reconnect with that part of herself that knew it wasn't right—to feel that discomfort in her body. Then I had to help her learn how to set boundaries. You might think, "Of course, that's wrong." But she didn't know. That's the point!

You never know how extreme a situation will become when a teen is disconnected from their inner knowing. The more connected they are to their intuition, the better decisions they will make. And the more authentic you are with them about your own feelings, the more you help them connect with their own—strengthening their trust in themselves.

By being honest about our struggles, we give our children permission to do the same. This deepens their connection to themselves and empowers them to make healthier choices. Isn't that what we truly want for our kids?

Ultimately, the more we examine our own patterns and

behaviors, the less we act out of unconscious wounds. Take the example of the mother who tells her child, "Nothing is wrong." She may have been raised to believe that expressing emotions is weak, dramatic, or negative. Her response isn't intentional—it's a learned behavior.

The key is recognizing these patterns so we don't project them onto our children. When we heal ourselves, we help them stay whole and healthy, too.

Take a few moments and reflect on these questions:

- *How have you been inauthentic in regards to what you feel?*
- *How do you support your teen being more intuitive?*
- *What are some behaviors you can develop to help them be more connected to themselves?*

RESPOND OR REACT

◆ SITUATION ◆
Your teen is in a relationship that doesn't seem healthy.

◆ REACTION ◆
Telling him that he is in an abusive relationship and convincing him he needs to break up with her, so you can feel safe. Not seeing this as his learning.

◆ POSSIBLE OLD BELIEFS ◆
I'm not in control of my life. I'm not safe in the world. I need to fix things. I need to protect. The unknown is scary. The worst will aways happen. I'm never heard.

◆ RESPONSE ◆
Always start with a deep breath and go inside and do your inner work. Trying to fix him is projecting your feelings. Ask him questions like, "What is it about your girlfriend's behavior that troubles you? Do you like the way your girlfriend treats you? What does she do that feels off to you? Do you believe there are girls out there that would treat you better? Do you think you deserve being treated better?" The more you remain calm, the better chance you have of helping him reflect on his own situation.

CHAPTER SIX

Communication, Can You Hear Me?

s it important to be able to communicate with your teen? I would assume your answer would be, "Of course." What does communication look like to you? I believe for most parents, communication looks like trying to get their point across to their teen to keep them safe. Yes, keeping your teen safe is really important, but if they are shut down to you and not hearing you, your advice lands on deaf ears, and safety is at an even greater risk.

Communicating through your fears, which comes from you being triggered and your old beliefs, doesn't work. If you are trying to convince them of your point of view to keep them safe, that is coming from your fears. Explore what old beliefs you are buying into, and again, go inward, pause, breathe, and don't project your fears onto your teen. Because as soon as you do, they will back up and resist anything you say. If you want your teen to stay open to you, get close to your old beliefs and triggers, and if you are activated, go inward, period!

The best way to communicate with your teen is to listen to them, actually hear what they are saying, and do your best to keep your fears out of the conversation. If you can keep your fears out of the conversation, your opinions and judgments will also stay on the sidelines. But if you do voice your opinions, it will land on your teen as a judgment.

The second you react, you shut your teen down and they stop listening, and then they are on their own for guidance because they can't—and won't—hear you anymore.

My grandson is 21, and I asked him a couple of years ago for a testimonial for my website about his mother, because she works with me and teens. I asked him some questions, and this is what he said:

"What makes my mom a good mother is how open and loving she is. Some parents say no for no reason; she opens it up for discussion and looks at the bigger picture of a situation, and we actually communicate. She is not quick to judge and lets me make mistakes, which helps me learn from those mistakes. Even though it might not be the best outcome, it's the best learning. She also gives me space to think about things and to work through them before we talk. She is a great listener and truly cares about what's going on in my life but not with intrusion, and this makes it easier to share."

This testimonial pretty much sums up how important this style of communication is. Another key point is that we need to let our teens make mistakes because when they experience the consequences of their mistakes, that's how they learn. Most people learn from their experiences in life, not from being told what to do or what not to do.

A mother I was mentoring said she didn't want her teen to make mistakes because she feared it was too dangerous. As you can see, her fears are completely guiding her approach in communicating with her teen. The reality is, her teen is going to make mistakes. We all make mistakes because we are human—we are imperfect beings. So, if you have a lot of fears around your teen making mistakes, you will be triggered all the time. Just don't project those fears onto your teen; go inward, look at what beliefs you are buying into, and sit with the feeling you have. It's difficult in those moments to sit with really uncomfortable feelings, but if you don't, you will project that discomfort onto your teen, pushing them away and shutting them down.

The more open they are to you, the more they will come to you for guidance, and the chances of them making dangerous decisions are far less than if they're out there on their own.

If you keep telling your kids, "Don't do this, don't do that," you are robbing them of a learning experience. If they can't experience situations in their life, how are they going to learn the lessons they need to learn? If you tell your teen, "Don't drink or do drugs," for example, do you think they will automatically listen to that advice? No. Because if your teen wants to do something, they will do it anyway. And if you are just telling them not to do something, you will make them defend a bad position. Even if it's not defending it to you, they will do it in their own mind. We never want to put them in a position where they must defend something that is not good for them. The consequences of their actions are usually enough to facilitate learning, although some people keep making the same mistakes over and over. I believe a teen is less likely to do that if they have a parent who communicates effectively.

If you have good communication with your teen and they are open to you, conversations about tough situations will be much easier. If they are going through a hard time and they know you will listen without judgment or fear, there is a better chance they will come to you, share what they are going through, and be able to move through their issues a lot faster with your guidance.

> *"The quality of your life is the quality of your communication."*
>
> — ANTHONY ROBBINS

A client of mine was hounding her daughter about not getting up in the morning early enough to get to school on time and about her grades dropping. She told her daughter that she was going to be homeless for the rest of her life if she didn't graduate from high school. After working with me, she realized how much her fears were influencing her parenting. She started to realize how big her fears were around her kids not being able to financially support themselves, and she started doing her inner work around her fears. She then went to her daughter calmly and explained her fears, saying that she had confidence in her daughter's ability to understand her own actions and consequences. She let her daughter know that if she needed anything, she was there. This approach doesn't mean you don't set boundaries about not going to school on time or getting poor grades. You still set boundaries (more on that in Chapter Seven).

Sometimes, we are a bigger distraction than a help to our teen. We take them away from figuring things out by reacting from our fears and harping on an issue. Instead of figuring out the issue for themselves, all they're thinking is, "My mom is driving me crazy with her nagging. I just want to get away from her."

This also applies when your teen comes to you with an issue, and you become more emotional about it than they are. I was mentoring a teen, and I was trying to encourage her to go to her mother about a situation, and she said she couldn't because her mother gets so emotional and can't handle it. This teen figured out early on that she had to handle her own problems because her mother would get more upset than she would. So, the mother unknowingly created a situation where her daughter wouldn't go to her with her issues.

Your child's communication development starts when they are born. How you communicate with them at an early age, will be how they communicate with you as teens. Something I often noticed with my daughter and grandson when he was young was that my daughter would always ask him questions without judgment and help him explore issues more without letting her own emotions cloud his thought process. By contrast, I see many parents condemning their kids for having an opinion, making them feel ashamed for asking questions. If you want an open relationship with your teen, they can't feel diminished or inferior when they come to you with questions or concerns.

Another good example of a communication breakdown happened with a teen I mentored. Kylie was pretending to be a good church-going teen so her parents would stay off her back and she could at least have a little bit of freedom. When I asked Kylie how this made her feel, she said, "Sad, because I feel like I don't have a relationship with my parents. I just feel like I'm being ruled." She had a lot of anger toward her parents. In this situation, it is tough for me to shift the family dynamics unless I have an opportunity to work with the parents. If the parents aren't willing to look at their own issues tied to their need to control their teen to mirror their beliefs, then she will always be disconnected from her parents and actually resent religion instead of embracing it. Without the pressure, she might have maintained her connection to God instead of resisting it and to her parents as well.

It's so important to manage our fears so we can communicate effectively and see our children as beings we are in a relationship with and treat them with the respect they deserve.

Take a few moments and reflect on these questions:

- ◆ *What does communication look like to you?*
- ◆ *How do you communicate through fear?*
- ◆ *Do you feel you are a good listener and what does this look like?*

RESPOND OR REACT

◆ SITUATION ◆

Your teen is way behind on a subject at school, and doesn't let you know. You find out from his teacher.

◆ REACTION ◆

Yelling at him about not telling you he was behind when you had asked about his homework. Grounding him and treating him poorly for a couple days because you're angry at him.

◆ POSSIBLE OLD BELIEFS ◆

I need to fix things. I'm not respected. I'm not considered. I'm always betrayed. I'm not heard. I'm responsible for others. Life is exhausting.

◆ RESPONSE ◆

Always go inside and do your inner work around what you were feeling about the situation. If you do nothing else to do this. Start with taking a pause and breathing. Yelling at him doesn't create an environment for learning. This is a great opportunity to teach him how to communicate and find out why he didn't. Ask him questions like: Why didn't you communicate about being so far behind? Use this as a chance to teach him about communication. When we punish through our own fears, we missed the opportunity to guide.

CHAPTER SEVEN

Boundaries—
A Framework for Growth

B reaking boundaries you set as a parent for your teen can be one of the most triggering aspects of your inner work. When a teen repeatedly disregards the rules of the household, it can stir up deep-seated beliefs such as, I'm not respected, I'm not in control, I can't trust people, I'm not considered, or I can't have boundaries. These feelings can quickly lead to reactive parenting, where emotions provoke reactions rather than thoughtful communication.

Before addressing any boundary violation with your teen, take a moment and do your inner work. Here are the steps to process any violation, allowing you to pause, reflect, and respond rather than react:

1. **Identify the Trigger.**
   Ask yourself: What about this situation is upsetting me the most? Is it the feeling of being disrespected, or not being in control, etc.? Try to take it off of your teen and see what is happening inside of you. The trigger should lead you to your old beliefs and feelings.

2. **Challenge Old Beliefs.**
   Where does this feeling come from? It is always rooted in
   past experiences, your own upbringing, or societal expectations. What old belief are you buying into? Even if it makes
   sense that you are in fear about your teen's safety, go
   inward first before you address the issue. Sometimes, we
   react strongly to our teens because their behavior rubs up
   against our wounding.

3. **Regulate Your Emotions—Be with Your Feelings**
   Before addressing the boundary violation, take a moment
   to breathe, step away if needed, and regain emotional
   balance by allowing yourself to be with your feelings. Don't
   project them onto your teen. Your ability to stay calm will
   directly influence how your teen responds. If they sense
   heightened emotions, they may shut down or go into
   defense mode.

4. **Approach with Curiosity, Not Control.**
   Instead of immediately enforcing a consequence, ask
   open-ended questions: What was going on for you when
   you made this choice? Help me understand why you didn't
   follow through with our agreement. This creates space for a
   conversation rather than a power struggle.

5. **Reinforce Boundaries with Collaboration.**
   Boundaries should not feel like punishments but rather
   agreements that support trust and respect in the household. Revisit the boundary together: How do we make sure
   this doesn't happen again? What consequence feels fair
   and makes sense? When your teen feels included in the

process, they are more likely to take ownership of their actions. Make sure to utilize an opportunity for learning from this mistake.

Boundaries are essential in every relationship, but when it comes to parenting teens, they serve as a foundation for trust, respect, and personal growth. Many parents assume that setting boundaries means enforcing strict rules, but boundaries are most effective when they are created with your teen, not for them.

A common struggle between parents and teens is the feeling of control—teens want independence, while parents want to ensure their safety. The key is to find a balance where boundaries provide guidance without making your teen feel powerless. When teens feel like they have a say in the rules and consequences that affect them, they are far more likely to respect and follow them.

Boundaries are not about punishment; they are about teaching responsibility, self-respect, and accountability. When done right, boundaries help teens develop essential life skills, such as decision-making, emotional regulation, and understanding natural consequences. Instead of creating an atmosphere of rebellion, setting boundaries together can help foster open communication and mutual understanding.

Let's explore why boundaries matter, how to establish them collaboratively, and how enforcing consequences with empathy can strengthen—not damage—your relationship with your teen.

Boundaries are often misunderstood, especially in parent-teen relationships. Many teens see them as rules imposed by controlling parents, while some parents feel that without strict boundaries, their teen would spiral into bad decision-making. But in reality, boundaries are not about control; they're about safety, trust, and mutual respect.

"Lack of boundaries invites lack of respect."

— ANONYMOUS

Just like adults, teens need boundaries to help them navigate the world, make good choices, and learn responsibility. The key to effective boundaries is collaboration. When boundaries are created with your teen, rather than for them, they are more likely to respect and follow them. This approach helps your teen feel empowered rather than ruled over, strengthening your relationship instead of creating resistance.

Why Boundaries Matter for Teens

1. **Boundaries Provide Security** – Clear expectations help teens feel safe, knowing there is structure in place.

2. **Boundaries Teach Responsibility** – Boundaries show teens that their actions have consequences, helping them develop self-discipline.

3. **Boundaries Foster Independence** – Learning to navigate boundaries prepares teens for adulthood, where they will need to set their own limits.

4. **Boundaries Encourage Trust** – When boundaries are set together, teens feel heard and respected, making them more likely to open up.

Setting Boundaries Together

Instead of imposing rules from a place of authority, try co-creating boundaries with your teen. Here's how:

1. **Start with a Conversation.**
   - Ask your teen what they think fair boundaries should be.
   - Share your own concerns and reasons for needing boundaries.
   - Make it a dialogue, not a lecture.

2. **Be Clear and Specific.**
   - Vague rules like "Be responsible" don't work. Instead, be clear:
     - "Be home by 10 PM on school nights."
     - "Phone is off and charging outside the bedroom by 9 PM."

3. **Agree on Consequences.**
   - Consequences should be reasonable and related to the boundary.
   - Example: If the agreed-upon curfew is 10 PM, and your teen repeatedly comes home late, a logical consequence might be an earlier curfew for a week—not taking away their phone for a month.
   - When teens help decide consequences, they take more ownership of their actions.

4. **Follow Through with Consistency and Empathy.**
   - If a boundary is broken, enforce the consequence calmly and consistently—not out of your fears and anger.
   - Acknowledge their feelings: "I know losing car privileges for a few days is frustrating, but we agreed that driving requires responsibility."

- Let them know mistakes are learning opportunities, not punishments.

Boundaries vs. Control

Teens naturally push against boundaries—it's part of their development. But when they feel included in decision-making, they are more likely to respect the structure. The goal isn't control, it's guidance. A teen who feels heard is more likely to come to you for advice, respect your rules, and build a healthy sense of self-discipline.

Teens need to have boundaries, too!

Teens also deserve respects and personal boundaries and as well. For instance, knocking on their bedroom door before entering shows consideration for their privacy. A teen once told me she wasn't allowed to have a lock on her door, and her father would enter whenever he wanted. This lack of personal space felt deeply dishonoring to her. While I completely understand the need to check phones or rooms if there is a genuine concern for safety, it's crucial to balance this with respect for their autonomy.

Another area to honor is when your teen asks for a moment to process their emotions. If they say they need space and aren't ready to talk, respect that. Continuing to push for resolution in the moment can backfire, causing more resistance rather than openness.

Teaching teens to honor boundaries starts with parents modeling that behavior. If you don't respect their limits, they may grow up accepting relationships where their boundaries are disregarded. This could impact their ability to confidently say, "No, that doesn't work for me." For example, if your daughter struggles to assert herself in a relationship, it may stem from an environment where she was never allowed to say no. Giving her the space to practice setting boundaries at home will empower her to do the same in future relationships.

Take a few moments and reflect on these questions:

- *What boundaries does your teen come up against that trigger you?*
- *Do you react or respond? How?*
- *What could you do differently?*
- *How do you dishonor your teens boundaries?*

RESPOND OR REACT

◆ SITUATION ◆
Your teen has a curfew that she consistently breaks.

◆ REACTION ◆
Nagging her to honor the curfew, saying she doesn't respect you, and laying a heavy consequence like grounding her for a month, acting out of your own frustrations.

◆ POSSIBLE OLD BELIEFS ◆
I'm not respected. I'm not heard. I can't have boundaries. I'm not considered. I need to fix things. I don't matter. I'm not important.

◆ RESPONSE ◆
Breathe and go inside and don't react out of your own frustrations and do your inner work around what is coming up for you. Start with taking a pause and breathing. Make sure you don't blame them for how you feel. Realize this is an opportunity for learning and you don't want to miss it due to being in your own emotions. If you can be in a place of calm while initiating consequences together, the outcome will be better.

CHAPTER EIGHT

Respect: A Two-Way Street

Respect, regard or consideration is a two-way street. If you do not have respect or regard for me, it will be hard for me to have respect or regard for you. Respect is often expected from teens but not always given in return. Many parents demand respect without realizing that true respect is built, not forced. It's easy to fall into the mindset of: "I'm the parent, so you must respect me." But respect is a mutual experience, and if teens don't feel respected, they often won't give it back.

"Respect is one of the greatest expressions of love."

— MIGUEL ANGEL RUIZ

An example of this came from a friend of mine who shared a story of when he was in school at the age of 43. His teacher didn't show him respect but would instead show respect to "this little 20-year-old twerp"—his words. I started asking him questions like: "Why do you think he didn't respect you?" and "Do you do anything in the class that might have bothered him?" It turned out that my friend was always late. When I asked him if the 20-year-old was ever late, he said no. I then challenged him, asking why he thought he deserved respect even though he hadn't earned it. He said it was because of his age. I pointed out that respect has nothing to do with age and everything to do with one's actions and how you treat others.

One of the biggest challenges in parent-teen relationships is the feeling of being dismissed. Teens want to be heard, and when they feel like their opinions don't matter or that they're constantly being corrected, they start to shut down. Respecting your teen doesn't mean you let them do whatever they want—it means you listen, consider their feelings, and guide them with fairness rather than control.

Here are some key ways to build a relationship based on respect:

- **Listen Without Interrupting** – When your teen is speaking, avoid jumping in with corrections or judgments. Let them express their thoughts fully before responding.
- **Acknowledge Their Feelings** – You don't have to agree with them, but validating their emotions shows that you care about their perspective. Saying "I can see why that upset you" can go a long way.
- **Model the Behavior You Want** – If you want respect, demonstrate it. Speak to your teen with kindness, even when you're frustrated. Avoid sarcasm, yelling, or dismissive comments.
- **Set Clear Expectations** – Respect doesn't mean no boundaries. Instead, explain the why behind your rules and be open to reasonable discussions about them.

◆ **Apologize When Necessary** – Parents make mistakes, too. If you lose your temper or say something unfair, owning up to it teaches your teen that respect includes accountability.

When respect is present on both sides, communication improves, trust grows, and conflicts become easier to navigate. A teen who feels respected is far more likely to return that respect, not just to their parents but in all their relationships.

Take a few moments and reflect on these questions:

- *In what ways do you think your teen would say you disrespect her/him?*
- *How do you react when they disrespect you?*
- *What could you do differently?*
- *How do you think your teen would feel if you were showing them more respect?*

RESPOND OR REACT

◆ SITUATION ◆

Your teen gets upset and yells at you and says she hates you.

◆ REACTION ◆

Yelling back and grounding her severely. Then get into
a screaming match with her.

◆ POSSIBLE OLD BELIEFS ◆

I'm not respected. I'm not considered. Life is exhausting.
I'm not in control of my life. I don't have rights. I'm not
appreciated. I can't have boundaries. I'm always doing
something wrong. I feel disconnected. I need to fix
things. I don't matter. I'm not important.

◆ RESPONSE ◆

The best thing to do is take a big breath and do the Inner
Work. Tell her you are triggered. Explain you are going to go
into the other room and get a hold of yourself because you
don't want to react in this way. First realize that she is triggered and that is why she behaved that way. Don't take it personally. After you have had a moment to do your inner work,
go back and apologize to your teen for yelling. Tell her you
want to show up for her, and allow her to have her feelings.
Ask if there is a way she might be able to express her feelings
without yelling and that you would like to do the same, and
maybe this is something you could practice together.

CHAPTER NINE

Honesty, Integrity, and the Power of Your Word

Honesty isn't just about telling the truth; it's about living in a way that aligns with your values. It's about keeping your word, being reliable, and acting with integrity—even when no one is watching. As parents, we want our teens to be honest, but are we modeling the same behavior?

The best way to raise an honest teen is to be an honest parent. If you model integrity, consistency, and the power of keeping your word, your teen will be much more likely to do the same. Honesty isn't just a rule—it's a value, a foundation, and a way of living that strengthens trust and deepens relationships.

The Power of Your Word

Your word holds weight. When you say you'll do something, whether it's picking your teen up on time, following through on a consequence, or simply being present when they need you, your ability to keep that commitment shapes how they see you and how they see themselves. If you frequently make promises but don't follow through, your teen learns that your words don't matter.

Teens notice inconsistencies. If we tell them honesty is important but then lie to get out of an obligation, what message are we really sending? If we expect them to own up to their mistakes but make excuses for our own, they'll likely do the same.

Integrity: Doing the Right Thing Even When It's Hard

Integrity isn't just about being honest—it's about being truthful and accountable. It's about making choices that reflect your values. For teens, this could mean standing up for a friend being bullied, or admitting when they've made a mistake. For parents, it's about acknowledging when we've been unfair, apologizing when necessary, and showing that honesty isn't just expected—it's practiced.

Creating an Environment Where Honesty Feels Safe

Many teens lie not because they're inherently dishonest, but because they fear the reaction of their parents. If honesty consistently leads to harsh punishment or shame, they'll learn to hide the truth instead of owning it. Instead of reacting with anger when they admit a mistake, consider saying:

- ◆ "I appreciate you telling me the truth. Let's figure out how to handle this together."
- ◆ "It took courage to admit that. That means a lot to me."
- ◆ "Thank you for being honest. Now let's talk about how to make this right."

When honesty is met with understanding and problem-solving rather than fear, teens are more likely to tell the truth.

Holding Yourself and Your Teen Accountable

Mistakes will happen—both for you and your teen. The goal isn't perfection; it's accountability. When a teen breaks a rule, the consequence should align with the action and be something they can learn from. Likewise, when we as parents mess up, owning our mistakes and making them right teaches our teens the true meaning of integrity.

> *"Live so that when your children think of fairness, caring, and integrity, they think of you."*
>
> — H. JACKSON BROWN, JR.

Your teen is always watching. Show them integrity through your actions, not just your words.

Take a few moments and reflect on these questions:

- *Do you apologize when in the wrong with your teen? If not, why?*
- *Do you keep your word to your teen? If not, why not?*
- *When your teen makes a mistake do you lead with punishment or an opportunity to learn?*

RESPOND OR REACT

◆ SITUATION ◆
You catch your teen in a lie.

◆ REACTION ◆
Getting triggered and letting your fear run the show
and punish them right out of the chute.

◆ POSSIBLE OLD BELIEFS ◆
I'm not respected. I can't trust people. People aren't safe
I'm not in control of my life. I have no rights. The worst will
always happen. I feel disconnected. I need to fix things.

◆ RESPONSE ◆
Breathe and pause and try to step into their reality. If you
are too triggered, do your inner work before talking to
them. After, when you are calm, ask questions about the
situation; what made them not tell the truth? Really try to
understand their point of view. Ask how they could have
handled the situation differently. Maybe a punishment isn't
as valuable as having a conscious conversation to
help them see things differently.

"Being honest may not get you a lot of friends, but it'll always get you the right ones."

— JOHN LENNON

Help your teen understand that being truthful attracts relationships built on trust and respect.

CHAPTER TEN

Mistakes: Opportunities for Growth, Not Just Punishment

A s parents, it's easy to see mistakes as something that must be corrected immediately. We often react with frustration, disappointment, or even punishment, thinking that it will teach our teen a lesson. But what if we shifted our perspective? What if mistakes were seen as an essential part of learning rather than something to fear or avoid?

> *"When you make a mistake, there are only three things you should ever do about it: admit it, learn from it, and don't repeat it."*
>
> — PAUL BEAR BRYANT

Teaching teens accountability will help them build confidence and resilience in life.

The Role of Mistakes in Growth

Take Sarah, for example. She's a high school sophomore who forgot to turn in an important project, which dropped her grade significantly. Her mom's first instinct was to ground her, take away her phone, and lecture her about responsibility. But instead, she sat down with Sarah and asked, "What happened?"

It turned out that Sarah had been feeling overwhelmed but was too afraid to ask for help. Instead of just punishing her, her mom helped her come up with a plan to manage her time better and help her get in touch with her feelings. Helping teens understand themselves helps them regulate, and when they are able to manage their emotions they are able to receive information clearly. The consequence was still there. Sarah had to talk to her teacher and accept a lower grade, but instead of feeling defeated, she learned more about herself and how to plan better for the future.

Mistakes are a natural part of development. Every successful person—whether in business, sports, relationships, or life in general—has made countless mistakes along the way. The difference is that they learned from them rather than letting mistakes define them. Teaching our teens that mistakes are opportunities for learning rather than sources of shame builds resilience, confidence, and important problem-solving skills.

How Parents Can Respond to Mistakes

Instead of reacting to your teen's mistakes with immediate punishment, try these steps for a better outcome:

1. **Pause and Reflect** – Before reacting, take a moment to ask yourself: What's going on inside of me? What beliefs am I buying into? What is the real lesson here for me and my teen? Is this a mistake that requires a consequence, or is this a teaching moment?

2. **Stay Calm and Open** — If you approach the situation with anger or harshness, your teen will likely shut down, get defensive, or feel ashamed. Instead, approach with curiosity: "I see this happened. Can we talk about what led to it?"

3. **Encourage Ownership** — Help your teen take responsibility without shame. Ask them:

   ◆ What do you think went wrong?
   ◆ What can you learn from this?
   ◆ How can you make it right?

4. **Teach Problem-Solving Skills** — If your teen forgets an assignment, breaks something, or makes a poor choice, guide them in finding a solution rather than simply handing down a punishment. Let them take an active role in fixing their mistake.

5. **Model Learning from Mistakes** — Be honest about your own mistakes. When parents admit their faults and show how they've grown, it teaches teens that imperfection is okay and learning never stops.

Balancing Consequences and Growth

Consequences should be tied to growth, ones that help your teen understand why the mistake matters and how to avoid repeating it. Some mistakes require setting new boundaries, especially if they affect others. But instead of focusing only on the punishment, focus on the lesson.

For instance, if a teen repeatedly misses curfew, instead of just grounding them, a parent could say, "I need to be able to trust that you'll be home when you say you will. Since that trust was broken, let's set an earlier curfew for a while, and then we'll revisit it." This way, the consequence is tied to building responsibility rather than just being a punishment.

The Power of Grace

Finally, remember that your teen is still learning. They are in the biggest learning curve of their life actually. If they feel like they are always being punished, they may start hiding their mistakes rather than learning from them. By balancing accountability with guidance and support, you create a safe space where your teen can grow into a responsible and resilient adult.

Mistakes are inevitable. Growth is a choice. Let's help our teens choose growth.

Take a few moments and reflect on these questions:

- *Do you usually hand down a punishment before exploring a chance to help your teen grow and learn from their mistakes?*
- *When your teen makes a mistake, what is your old belief you are buying into?*
- *Do you apologize when you make a mistake?*

RESPOND OR REACT

◆ SITUATION ◆
Your teen calls you to pick her up because
she drank at a party.

◆ REACTION ◆
Getting triggered and yelling at her for drinking
and tell her she is grounded for a month.

◆ POSSIBLE OLD BELIEFS ◆
I'm not respected. I'm not heard. I'm not in control of my
life. I can't trust people. The worst will always happen. I
need to fix things.

◆ RESPONSE ◆
Breathe, pause and realize this is an opportunity
to show up for them calmly and teach them, not through
your emotions. First thank them for not driving after drinking and calling you. If you are too triggered, just go pick
them up and tell them you can talk about the situation
tomorrow. Do your inner work before talking to them.
When you are calm, realize the reality of the situation—
do you want them drinking and driving? Do you think telling them not to drink will guarantee they won't drink? Look
at the situation with a level head, not a triggered mind.

CHAPTER ELEVEN

Security and Self-Confidence: Building a Strong Foundation

S ecurity and self-confidence are two of the greatest gifts we can give our teens. When a teen feels secure in their home environment, they are more likely to develop confidence in themselves. But what does security really mean? It's more than just providing food, shelter, and clothing—it also includes emotional security. It's about a teen knowing they can come to you without fear of judgment, that they are loved even when they make mistakes, and that your love is not conditional regarding their performance or behavior.

> *"Behind every young child who believes in themselves is a parent who believed first."*
>
> — MATTHEW JACOBSON

Your belief in your teen's potential lays the foundation for their confidence.

Being secure and self-confident is critical in today's world. It's a lot tougher to be a secure teen today than it ever has been. My mentoring business has completely shifted over the

last four years. I've noticed that instead of the typical teen having high anxiety some of the time, it's more like most of them
have anxiety all of the time. This is why it is so important for
us to create a secure environment and the safety of our own
home, because it's hard to feel that secure in the outside world.

Creating a Secure Environment

Security comes from consistency. When parents are unpredictable—exploding one moment and calm the next—teens walk on
eggshells, unsure of what to expect. This erodes their sense of
safety. A secure home is one where:

- **Rules and expectations are clear** – Your teen should
  know what is expected of them and what the consequences are when expectations aren't met.
- **Love is unwavering** – They need to know that even
  when they fail or make mistakes, your love for them
  does not change.
- **Their voice matters** – When teens feel heard and
  valued, they develop confidence in their own thoughts
  and feelings.
- **They are allowed to express their feelings** – When
  feelings are stuffed, they can be internalized, resulting
  in depression.

The Link Between Security and Self-Confidence

A secure teen is more likely to be a confident teen. Confidence
isn't about arrogance or believing they are better than others—
it's about self-trust. A confident teen believes in their ability to

handle challenges, make decisions, and navigate the world.

How do parents help build confidence?

- **Encourage effort, not just outcomes** – Praise your teen for trying, even if they don't succeed. This teaches resilience.
- **Allow them to make choices** – Let them have input in decisions affecting them. This builds decision-making skills and self-trust.
- **Support, don't rescue** – If they forget their homework, resist the urge to rush it to school. Let them face natural consequences so they learn responsibility.

Confidence in Parents = Confidence in Teens

Your teen is watching you. If you doubt yourself, constantly seek approval, or put yourself down, they will absorb that. You model confidence when you:

- Speak kindly about yourself.
- Own your mistakes without shame.
- Stand firm in your decisions while being open to discussion.

A teen who feels secure will grow into a confident adult. Your job isn't to make their path easy but to provide a strong foundation where they feel safe to explore, make mistakes, and develop a strong belief in themselves. Confidence is built, not gifted, and it starts with the security you provide in your relationship.

Take a few moments and reflect on these questions:

- *What actions do you take to create security in your home?*
- *What things might you do that don't support security?*
- *In what areas of your life are you secure or insecure?*

RESPOND OR REACT

◆ SITUATION ◆

Your teen feels anxious about not being popular in school.

◆ REACTION ◆

Telling her how great she is and what a wonderful person she is, and that kids at school don't know anything!

◆ POSSIBLE OLD BELIEFS ◆

The worst will always happen. I need to fix things. I'm inadequate. I need to protect. I'm always doing something wrong.

◆ RESPONSE ◆

Breathe and do your inner work, and then look at your behaviors and what you might be doing to support a lack of confidence in your teen and yourself. Telling her she is great won't make her feel great.

CHAPTER TWELVE

Positivity Versus Negativity

Gratitude and positivity are powerful tools for shaping our lives, but they should never come at the expense of authentic emotions—especially for teens. As parents, we often want to encourage our children to "look on the bright side," to focus on what's good, and to maintain a positive outlook. While this is valuable, it's just as important to allow space for real, sometimes painful emotions to arise.

Teens are navigating intense emotions—joy, frustration, anxiety, excitement, sadness—often all at once. If we push them to always "stay positive" or rely on the law of attraction to override their struggles, we risk invalidating their experiences. Feelings don't disappear just because we want them to. They need to be acknowledged, processed, and moved through naturally in their own time.

A more balanced approach is to teach teens that it's okay to feel whatever comes up while also guiding them toward gratitude and perspective when they're ready.

- **Listen without fixing**– Let them vent, cry, or express frustration without immediately offering solutions or a "silver lining."

- **Validate their emotions** – Instead of saying, "Don't be upset," try, "That seems like a really tough situation."
- **Model gratitude** – Share how you practice gratitude in your own life, without forcing them to do the same in the moment.
- **Encourage emotional awareness** – Help them recognize their emotions without judgment and show them how to move toward a more positive space when they're ready.

The goal isn't to dwell in negativity, nor is it to force artificial positivity. It's about balance—teaching teens that all emotions are valid and that they have the ability to shift their perspective when the time is right. When they see that feeling deeply and being grateful can coexist, they'll develop the resilience and self-awareness they need to navigate life in a healthy way.

Take a few moments and reflect on these questions:

- *Does it make you uncomfortable when your teen expresses feeling of unhappiness?*
- *What old beliefs are you buying into when they show emotions that make you feel uncomfortable?*
- *When do you discount your teen and try to get them to see things more positively?*
- *Do you move through life avoiding or suppressing your feelings?*
- *What do you do when you feel unhappy?*

RESPOND OR REACT

◆ SITUATION ◆

Your teen is devastated about her boyfriend breaking up
with her and starting to date one of her girlfriends.

◆ REACTION ◆

Getting triggered and telling her he's not worth having
for a boyfriend if he did that, and to be glad you're
not with him anymore.

◆ POSSIBLE OLD BELIEFS ◆

I need to protect. People aren't safe. I'm not in control
of my life. The worst will always happen. I need to fix
things. Life isn't fair.

◆ RESPONSE ◆

Breathe and pause and try to step into her reality.
If you are too triggered, do your inner work first before
responding. Then, just explore how she is feeling by asking
questions or simply saying how difficult that would be...
I'm so sorry. Let her express her feelings, and put
yours on the shelf and deal with them later.

CHAPTER THIRTEEN

Teen Sexuality: Do You Contract Around Talking About Sex?

One of the biggest questions to ask yourself is: Do you find yourself avoiding or struggling to discuss sex with your teen? If you do not have an open dialogue about this topic, your teen will likely turn to other sources—peers, the internet, or media—to get their information. Without your guidance, they may receive misinformation or develop unhealthy views about sexuality.

It's essential to do your own inner work regarding sexuality so you can show up for your teen in a healthy, supportive way. If you have unresolved trauma, such as childhood sexual abuse or exposure to inappropriate sexual behaviors, you may unconsciously project these issues onto your teen. This can manifest in two ways:

- **Avoidance** –You completely ignore the topic, leaving your teen without guidance.
- **Overcompensation** – You talk about it too much, possibly in an inappropriate or overwhelming way.

Your role is to clean up your own "mess" in this area so you don't pass it on to your teen.

Recognizing Your Triggers

If discussing sex with your teen makes you uncomfortable or reactive, it's important to ask yourself why. Take time to reflect on the emotions that surface:

- Are you feeling anxious, angry, or judgmental?
- Do you find yourself shutting down the conversation?
- Are you imposing your personal fears onto them?

Your teen needs a calm and informed parent who can provide guidance, not someone who reacts emotionally. Addressing your own blocks around sexuality will help you become a safe, approachable resource for your teen.

A Powerful Exercise in Awareness

When my oldest daughter was 14 years old, I sat by the pool with her and two of her friends. I asked them, "If you were pregnant today, what would you do?"

At first, they were shocked. Then, one by one, they answered:

- "I would have the baby and give it up for adoption."
- "I would have an abortion."
- "I would keep the baby."

I couldn't have asked for better answers. Rather than leaving it at that, I opened a discussion about each choice.

- The girl who was for adoption explained why she thought that option wasn't that great.
- The girl for abortion shared her reasons why she felt it wasn't a good choice.
- The girl who would keep the baby realized that wasn't a very good choice either.

By the end of the conversation, they all realized that none of the options was ideal, and they came to a powerful conclusion: the risk of pregnancy after sex wasn't worth it. This exercise helped them see the real-world consequences of having sex and made them feel the weight of their choices in a way no lecture could.

This type of conversation can also be adapted for boys, helping them understand the gravity of their responsibility in preventing pregnancy.

Empowering Your Teen to Make Their Own Decisions

The goal is not to scare or control your teen but to help them make informed decisions. If they feel like they are the ones choosing to wait or set boundaries, they will be more committed to their choice. If they simply hear, "Don't have sex," they may ignore the advice.

Your job is to educate, support, and empower them. When they have a strong sense of self, they can confidently say: "No, thank you—that doesn't work for me."

When a decision comes from a place of confidence and self-assurance, it is rarely questioned or challenged. The way we guide our teens always starts with us—are we doing our inner work so we can show up from a place of calm rather than panic? If we remain contracted and triggered, conversations about sexuality will feel awkward or may not happen at all. If you find yourself reacting emotionally when discussing this topic, take a step back, look inward, and ask yourself why. Your job is not to project your unresolved feelings onto your teen, but to provide them with the space, clarity, and support they need.

Take a few moments and reflect on these questions:

- *Is sex a tabu subject in your house, and why?*
- *What comes up for you when this topic is discussed?*
- *Have you explored sexual abuse in your past and resolved it? If not how might it show up with your kids?*

RESPOND OR REACT

◆ SITUATION ◆

Your son is asking for his girlfriend to spend the night.

◆ REACTION ◆

Getting triggered and telling them they are crazy if they think this is going to happen and shut down the conversation.

◆ POSSIBLE OLD BELIEFS ◆

I'm not respected. I'm not heard. I'm not in control of my life. I have no rights. The worst will always happen. I need to fix things.

◆ RESPONSE ◆

Breathe and pause and try to step into their reality. If you are too triggered, do your inner work before talking to them. After, when you are calm, ask questions about the situation; why this is important to them and really step into their reality. This is a very personal matter, with each family being different and no answer is either right or wrong. It's just important to handle it through the highest place inside you, not your triggered place.

CHAPTER FOURTEEN

Navigating the Digital Jungle

The digital world is vast, ever-expanding, and full of both opportunities and dangers. For parents, the challenge lies in striking a balance, allowing teens the freedom to explore and connect while maintaining appropriate boundaries to keep them safe. But just like in every other aspect of parenting, this begins with self-awareness. Before we impose rules on our teens, we must check in with our own fears, ensuring we are setting boundaries from a place of wisdom rather than anxiety.

Setting Healthy Limits Without Controlling

The reality is, screens are a major part of our kids' lives. From social interactions to school assignments, technology is woven into their daily experience. But just because screens are necessary doesn't mean their use should be unlimited

Boundaries around screen time should be intentional and based on the well-being of the child, rather than a reaction to our own discomfort around the behavior of our teen.

Practical ways to set healthy limits include:

- **Family Tech Agreements** – Sit down as a family and create a technology contract that includes screen-free zones (such as mealtimes and bedtime) and screen limits that allow for balance.
- **Device-Free Time** – Model and encourage device-free periods where the entire family takes a break from screens to foster real-life connections.
- **Parental Control Programs** – Utilize apps and settings to block inappropriate content, limit screen time, and set usage restrictions. These programs allow parents to monitor without micromanaging.
- **Lead by Example** – If we want our teens to have a healthy relationship with technology, we must demonstrate the same. If we are constantly on our phones, they will likely mirror that behavior.

Privacy vs. Safety: Walking the Fine Line

Many parents struggle with how much privacy to give their teen online. The key here is to respect their growing independence while also ensuring their safety.

- **Trust, but Verify** – While we want to trust our teens, it's also important to have safeguards in place. Let them know upfront that you reserve the right to check in if necessary—not to invade their privacy, but to ensure their well-being.
- **Open Communication over Surveillance** – Instead of obsessively monitoring their every move, foster open conversations about their online world. Ask about the

apps they use, their digital friendships, and their experiences.

- **Have a 'Red Flag' Policy** – Let your teen know that if you ever feel they are in danger—whether from cyberbullying, inappropriate content, or unsafe online relationships—you will step in.

Checking in with Yourself First

One of the biggest mistakes we can make is parenting out of fear rather than wisdom. When it comes to technology, we often project our own anxieties onto our kids—whether it's fear of addiction, exposure to harmful content, or social isolation. While these concerns are valid, reacting out of fear can cause unnecessary conflict and make our teens more resistant to our guidance.

When we acknowledge our fears instead of projecting them, we create space for genuine connection and problem-solving. Our goal is not to control our teens' digital lives but to equip them with the tools they need to navigate it wisely.

I've noticed that many parents fear their teen will feel excluded if they aren't on social media. Too often, parents prioritize keeping their child happy over making decisions that serve their child's best interests. Instead of avoiding discomfort by giving in, take a step back and examine your own fears. Do the inner work necessary to separate your anxieties from what is truly best for your teen.

Empowering Teens to Self-Regulate

Rather than simply imposing restrictions, we should also teach our teens to manage their own screen time and online presence. Some ways to encourage self-regulation include:

- **Helping Them Set Their Own Limits** – Ask them how much screen time they think is reasonable and work together on boundaries.
- **Discussing Digital Well-Being:** Talk about how excessive screen time can impact their sleep, mental health, and real-life relationships.
- **Encouraging Digital Detoxes:** Normalize taking breaks from social media and screens to recharge.

Navigating the digital world is not about policing our teens but about guiding them. By setting healthy boundaries, fostering trust, and managing our own fears, we create an environment where they can learn to make responsible digital choices.

We don't have to fear technology—we just have to parent through it with intention, self-awareness, and a commitment to staying connected to our teen.

Take a few moments and reflect on these questions:

- *What exactly am I afraid of?*
- *Is my fear rooted in a real risk, or is it an assumption?*
- *Am I setting this boundary for their well-being or to ease my own anxiety.*
- *How can I communicate my concerns without making them feel controlled?*

RESPOND OR REACT

◆ SITUATION ◆

Your son is on his phone all of the time and when you tell him to get off he has a meltdown and starts yelling.

◆ REACTION ◆

Getting triggered and putting all these strong rules in place, and when he keeps acting out, you give in and let him have his way.

◆ POSSIBLE OLD BELIEFS ◆

I'm not respected. I'm not heard. I'm not in control of my life. I have not rights. The worst will always happen. I need to fix things. Life is exhausting.

◆ RESPONSE ◆

Breathe and pause. If you are too triggered, do your inner work before talking to them. After, when you are calm, let him know that limits on how much he uses his device are important. Ask him how much time he thinks he should be able to use his device and can you both come up with a plan together? That unlimited use is not an option. It's critical to have these conversations through the highest place inside you, not your triggered place. If he is still being unreasonable, tell him you are going to shut down the phone until he is ready to have a calm conversation. And do it!

CHAPTER FIFTEEN

Rebuilding Trust

s your teen shut down and distant? If so, rebuilding trust will take time and patience. It's important to reflect on the lessons in the previous chapters and examine how your fears and old beliefs shape your reactions. Are you responding from a place of love and understanding, or are you operating from fear and control? The way you show up in your relationship with your teen directly impacts their willingness to be open with you. Trust cannot be forced; it must be nurtured.

I mentored a mother whose daughter was totally upsetting the dynamics of the family. I worked with the mother on shifting her old beliefs and detaching from the behavior of the preteen, through love. I actually never even talked to the preteen. After about three months of the mother working on the things that triggered her and changing those behaviors and beliefs, her daughter's behavior started shifting as well. The mother said it was miraculous.

"Trust takes years to build, seconds to break, and forever to repair."

— UNKNOWN

Teach your teen that trust is "precious and must be handled with care.

If you want to have an influence on your kids you need to have an open relationship with them, which means they have to trust you. When we look at our triggers and go inward and do our inner work, we start to show up in a more loving way for our teens, and this is what opens them up to you. Be the observer of yourself and the destructive behaviors that keep the wedge between you and your teen.

Why Trust Gets Broken

Trust between parents and teens can break down for many reasons, including:

- **Inconsistency** – Saying one thing but doing another, such as setting rules you don't follow yourself.
- **Harsh Reactions** – If your teen is afraid of your reaction, they'll stop opening up.
- **Judgment** – Criticizing their choices, appearance, or opinions instead of listening with an open mind.
- **Control Overload** – Making all the decisions without allowing them to have a say.
- **Lack of Follow Through** – If you make promises and don't keep them, they learn not to trust your word.
- **Not Owning Mistakes** – Parents make mistakes, too. If you never apologize or take responsibility, they may feel unheard and resentful.

How to Start Rebuilding Trust

If trust has been broken, don't panic—it's repairable with consistent effort. Here are some steps to begin:

1. Model What You Want to See

Teens learn from example. If you want them to be open, honest, and respectful, you have to show them what that looks like.

- Speak to them with the same respect you expect from them.
- Apologize when you mess up. Saying "I was wrong" teaches them accountability.
- Stay calm when discussing tough topics—your reaction determines how safe they feel opening up.

2. Give Them a Safe Space to Be Honest

If teens feel like telling the truth will get them in trouble or lead to a lecture, they'll avoid being honest.

- Instead of reacting immediately, ask, "What made you feel that way?" or "Help me understand why you made that choice."
- Focus on problem-solving instead of punishment.
- If they confess to something, thank them for being honest before addressing the issue.

3. Show Up Consistently

Teens will test if they can trust you before they open up. You build trust one interaction at a time.

- Keep your word, even with small things.

- Be available when they need you—not just when it's convenient.
- Check in without pushing. A simple, "I'm here if you want to talk," goes a long way.

4. Focus on Connection Over Control

The goal isn't to control your teen but to guide them while maintaining a strong relationship.

- Include them in decision-making about rules and consequences.
- Respect their boundaries, just as you want them to respect yours.
- Let go of power struggles. Ask yourself, "Is my reaction about them, or about my own fears?"

5. Be Patient

Rebuilding trust takes time, especially if there's been conflict in the past.

- Celebrate small wins—every open conversation is progress.
- If they don't open up right away, keep showing up with love and consistency.
- Trust the process—change won't happen overnight, but your efforts will make a difference.

Rebuilding trust isn't about making your teen change—it's about doing your inner work and watching the changes happen organically.

If you want to positively influence your teen, they need to trust you. And trust comes from feeling emotionally safe. When we take responsibility for our own emotional triggers and commit to doing our inner work, we begin to interact with our teens in a calmer, more loving way. This creates the safety they need to open up.

Take a few moments and reflect on these questions:

- *How can you show up for your teen to help heal the relationship and build trust?*
- *How do you lead with fear instead of love?*
- *Are you good at being the observer of your behaviors? How?*
- *What behaviors do you have that you wouldn't want your teen to learn from you?*

RESPOND OR REACT

◆ SITUATION ◆
Your teen is acting indifferent to you.

◆ REACTION ◆
Thinking it's about you and telling them their behavior
is unacceptable.

◆ POSSIBLE OLD BELIEFS ◆
I need to fix things. I'm always doing something wrong.
I'm rejected. I'm not special. I'm not loveable.
Love is hard to get.

◆ RESPONSE ◆
Take a deep breath and realize his behavior may not
have anything to do with you and let go of the stories
you have created in your head. Give your teen some
space, and do your inner work around how you feel. Take
it off of them and look at how you feel—sad, hurt,
or maybe lonely. Stay in your own lane and don't try
to get him to fix how you feel.

CHAPTER SIXTEEN

Healing Yourself and Your Children – It's All about You

Parenting is a job that takes more skill than most people realize or have developed yet. All it takes is the willingness to go to those uncomfortable places within ourselves to start the ball rolling. There is no room for judgment on this journey; there is only room for acceptance—acceptance of ourselves and acceptance of others.

We have relationships in our life for a reason; there is a bigger purpose to our existence. Our evolution depends on healing our wounds. If we don't look at those parts of us that need healing, we mostly end up hoping for someone else to fill that wounded place in us. Or we project our unresolved emotions onto others, expecting them to make us feel happy and whole. When we do our work to heal those wounds, it helps us love ourselves, and therefore allows us to go out into the world whole, with a better sense of who we are and help our teens do the same.

Isn't this our goal for our children? To help them have a better sense of themselves so they can be confident, resilient, and authentically happy?

This is an inside job, and if you want to heal your relationship with your kids, you must first start healing yourself. The beauty of this is that it's a lifelong journey, and we are all on that journey—either consciously or unconsciously. You can start the healing process within yourself at the same time you begin mending your connection with your teen.

This is about showing up for yourself in a whole new way—healing the deep wounds within so that you can be fully present for yourself and your teen in a more conscious, loving, and supportive way.

At the very heart of raising a strong, independent, and emotionally healthy teen is you. Your ability to understand yourself—your childhood story, your triggers, your fears, and your beliefs—directly impacts how you show up as a parent. The more inner work you do, the more you can guide your teen with clarity, love, and authenticity, rather than reacting from unresolved wounds.

Your teen needs the space to be themselves. Authenticity starts at home—when you model honesty, integrity, and self-acceptance, you give them permission to embrace their own identity without fear or shame. Open and respectful communication builds trust, while clear boundaries teach them self-respect and how to navigate relationships in a healthy way. Mistakes are inevitable, both for you and for them, but mistakes are also powerful teachers. The goal isn't perfection—it's learning, growing, and strengthening the bond between you.

As your teen explores their independence, security and confidence become their greatest assets. Your role isn't to control them but to support them in making decisions with self-awareness and conviction. Conversations around sexuality, trust, and responsibility are easier when you've done your inner work—when you're able to respond instead of react, educate instead of impose, and guide instead of judge.

Ultimately, good parenting isn't about fixing or changing your teen—it's about evolving yourself. The more you heal, the more you create a space where your teen feels safe to grow into the best version of themselves. Doing your inner work ensures that you're not projecting your fears, wounds, or unresolved emotions onto them. It allows them to navigate their world with confidence, resilience, and a strong sense of self.

Because in the end, the greatest gift you can give your teen is a parent who is whole, aware, and at peace with themselves.

Hello parents, I am deeply committed to supporting you on your journey to becoming the best parent you can be—especially through the rollercoaster ride of the teenage years. While this book focuses on parenting teens, the insights and tools within can benefit parents of children at any age. My hope is that these strategies feel simple, practical, and accessible, helping you navigate the challenges of parenting with confidence. While parenting is undoubtedly complex, the most rewarding part of this journey is the opportunity to truly know yourself. When you do, parenting becomes a more natural and intuitive process.

If you have a teenage daughter, don't forget to check out my book *My Feet Aren't Ugly, A Girls Guide to Loving Herself from the Inside Out*. I also do Mother-Daughter Retreats, mentoring, and I have online courses for both parents and teens. Check out my website and courses that follow.

- www.EmpoweredTeensandParents.com
- Debra@EmpoweredTeensandParents.com
- https://empoweredteensandparents.com/connect-with-your-teen/
- https://empoweredteensandparents.com/teen-self-esteem-4-weeks/

For Adult Mother Daughter, Couples and Individuals:

- www.SedonaSoulRetrieval.com
- Debra@SedonaSoulRetrieval.com

OTHER HELPFUL RESOURCES

- *My Feet Aren't Ugly, A Girl's Guide to Loving Herself from the Inside Out,* Debra Beck
- *Codependent No More,* Melody Beattie
- *When Things Fall Apart,* Pema Chodron
- *Welcome the Unwelcome,* Pema Chodron
- *A New Earth,* Eckhart Tolle
- *Untethered Soul,* Michael Singer
- *The Surrender Experiment,* Michael Singer
- *Waking the Tiger,* Peter Levine
- *Shadow Work,* Debbie Ford
- *Awareness,* Anthony De Mello
- *When The Body Says No,* Gabor Mate, MD
- *Enchanted Love,* Marianne Williamson
- *A Return to Love,* Marianne Williamson
- *Mother Hunger,* Kelly McDaniel
- *How to Love,* Thich Nhat Hanh
- *You Can Heal Your Life,* Louise Hay
- *Parenting Teens with Love & Logic,* Foster Cline
- *Life Without ED,* Jenni Schaefer (eating disorders)

Remember Debra's award-winning book for teen girls and her online courses for parents!

For Parents — To have a better understanding of what life is like for your teen and how your interactions are critical to your connections with your teen:
https://empoweredteensandparents.com/connect-with-your-teen/

For Teens — To have an understanding of themselves, so they can go out into the world confident and secure and participate with greatness:
https://empoweredteensandparents.com/teen-self-esteem-4-weeks/